J.J. Watt: The Inspiring Story of One of Football's Greatest Defensive Ends

An Unauthorized Biography

By: Clayton Geoffreys

Visit my website at www.claytongeoffreys.com
Cover photo by Jeffrey Beall is licensed under CC BY 2.0 / modified from original

Table of Contents

Foreword

When anyone thinks of the best defensive players in the National Football League today, it does not take long before someone says J.J. Watt. J.J. Watt has quickly emerged as one of the premier defensive players to play professional football, with a ridiculous ability to stop the greatest offensive players and quarterbacks. It should come as no surprise that Watt has won several defensive player of the year awards at this point in his career. Thank you for purchasing *J.J. Watt: The Inspiring Story of One of Football's Greatest Defensive Ends*. In this unauthorized biography, we will learn J.J.'s incredible life story and impact on the game of football. Hope you enjoy and if you do, please do not forget to leave a review!

Also, check out my website at claytongeoffreys.com to join my exclusive list where I let you know about my latest books. To thank you for your purchase, you can go to my site to download a free copy of *33 Life*

Lessons: Success Principles, Career Advice & Habits of Successful People. In the book, you'll learn from some of the greatest thought leaders of different industries on what it takes to become successful and how to live a great life.

Visit me at www.claytongeoffreys.com

Introduction

In an interview with the Houston Chronicle prior to the Houston Texans facing Cincinnati Bengals, who were undefeated at the time, on November 16, 2015 – Texans' defensive end J.J. Watt was answering questions before a big game. He was already well-known for having a number of tackles and sacks against some of the NFL's most elite players, including Andy Dalton; four games before this one gave Watt 18 total tackles and two sacks, along with one interception return for a touchdown in the AFC playoffs in 2011.

So reporters asked Watt about how he was able to get to Dalton, who was only 1-3 against Houston all-time. Was it his awareness of how they faced each other in college during the 2011 Rose Bowl between Watt's Wisconsin Badgers and Dalton's Texas Christian Horned Frogs? Was it hours of study? No, the answer was quite simple.

"I don't study quarterbacks like that. I just go get 'em." Watt said during the interview.

It seems like it's quite a basic answer, but it's enough of one. How else could you explain someone who had more than 300 tackles, more than 60 sacks, and who created several turnovers? With nearly a century of history that has produced thousands of household names for each of the various positions on both offense and defense, there are only a few players in the National Football League who can match the energy of J.J. Watt. However, beyond the Sundays where he puts on his Houston Texans uniform, there are few men like J.J. Watt – especially when you go back to his upbringing during his childhood.

Few people ever have their perfect future set when they are in the fourth grade and still pursue it through high school and college. There are also only a few people who would leave a college scholarship, which was at a mid-major college football program, to try and walk onto the college football team you grew up watching since childhood. The thing about J.J. Watt is that he has taken chances to pursue his dreams and, despite the high odds of not taking a place, he succeeded.

He has not only succeeded in being a dominant player in high school in a small town in Wisconsin, but also for the University of Wisconsin and now playing in the NFL with the Houston Texans. The thing that has always stood out about Watt is that while he remains high tempo in his energy, he's also remained equally focused in whatever he does, whether it's being a leader on the football field or being a positive role model and using his fame to make a positive impact in the community.

The beginnings of Watt's path to the NFL started very humbly in a small town of Pewaukee, Wisconsin, where he was in high school with a lot less muscle mass than he has now. He played tight end and defensive end as an Ironman athlete for football, which got him some letters of interest from smaller mid-major college programs like Northern Illinois University and Central Michigan University. While he signed with CMU, his heart was still in Wisconsin and he left college to try to save up to pursue playing for the Badgers at Camp Randall Stadium in Madison, Wisc. He was always told by many in his city that he was crazy since it was such a daunting task, just like his goals of playing in the NFL, a dream that he first announced to his fourth-grade teacher. Unlikely, yes. Impossible, no.

Watt would walk on as a transfer student to Wisconsin and was redshirted. He put in the time, hard work, and dedication to study film, learn the plays, and keep improving physically. By the time he made his first start in front of 80,000 home fans – wearing the classic red and white uniform – Watt was six-foot-five and filled out to about 290 pounds. He would be a terrorizing defensive end in the Big Ten Conference for his sophomore and junior seasons with the Badgers that included a trip to the 2011 Rose Bowl against Texas Christian University, where he faced someone who would become a familiar foe after college in quarterback Andy Dalton.

Watt brought that same desire to be great to the National Football League and was a first-round selection by the Houston Texans. Fans booed and few people were happy to hear about his selection as they wanted Nick Fairley, a highly rated defensive tackle who was coming out of Auburn University after winning a National Championship with the Tigers. Similar to when people told the young Watt that his dreams of playing football professionally were highly unlikely and doubted that he could do it, he would prove his doubters wrong in Houston and make them believers.

However, Watt would become one of the most dominant defensive ends in the game and was able to accumulate a large number of tackles for losses and sacks while also creating a number of turnovers. In addition to creating havoc for opposing quarterbacks and running backs, Watt is also one of a very few defensive linemen to have scored a touchdown in the NFL. We're not talking about the 80-yard interception return for a touchdown that he had back in 2014 against the Buffalo Bills, or the 45-yard fumble return for a touchdown against AFC South Division rivals Indianapolis Colts that same season. The 2014 season also saw Watt make three touchdown passes as a tight end, which he played high school and during his freshman season at Central Michigan University.

The one thing that has remained constant through Watt's playing career is that if you think he isn't able to do something, he's going to likely go out and prove you wrong. Whether it's being able to successfully walk onto a big-name NCAA Division 1 football program like Wisconsin, be drafted in the first round of the NFL Draft, or become one of the best defensive linemen in the history of the game without having missed a single start since starting his rookie season in 2011. Watt is a physical player who plays at a high tempo and has said in media interviews that he will keep playing until he can't do it anymore. At the rate that his statistics have continued to grow season after season, it might be a long time before fans start to notice any form of skill decline in J.J. Watt.

Watt doesn't plan on being known only for being a freak of nature on the football field. He's also taken a different responsibility very seriously: becoming a role model to young football fans who want to achieve success like he has done. Whether it's visiting children who are sick in a hospital, meeting those who actively serve in the United States Armed Forces, or helping to raise money to support after-school programs, Watt has embraced just about every facet of being a successful and positive professional football player because of his hard work, dedication, and his ethics that were formed by his family while growing up in the Midwest.

Chapter 1: Childhood and Early Life

Justin James Watt was born on March 22, 1989, in Waukesha, Wisconsin, a small suburb of Milwaukee in the southeastern part of the state. His dad John was a firefighter for the local department while his mother Connie was a stay-at-home parent. Watt had two younger brothers, T.J. and Derek, both of whom would also move on to play football and earn scholarships at the University of Wisconsin, although they never had the opportunity to play on the same field as their older brother J.J. Yet all three brothers were very close and played in the yard often – not just football, but other sports as well.

It also helped to have an expanded backyard that neighborhood children could share in the family's home in Pewaukee, which is a much smaller town than where Watt was born and had closer to 10,000 residents. In a Houston Chronicle interview back in

2012, Watt reflected on their home having a large backyard with no fences or trees that separated theirs from another two houses down, forming one giant yard that was perfect for youths to play football on.

All it took was running to each of the neighbor's doors to see if the children wanted to join the Watt brothers for a game of football, which was observed by Watt's mother would watch from a distance. Growing up, Watt played all different types of sports, not limiting himself to just playing on the football field with his brothers. In fact, the younger Watt was involved with one of the more popular sports in the state – hockey. A majority of the northern Midwest states have developed a passion for hockey and Watt started playing at the age of three. Over time, he would play well enough to play on travel teams that included trips to Canada multiple times and even over to Germany for a 10-day tournament.

In a story on NHL.com from 2013, he explained how playing hockey in Wisconsin was a tight-knit community. "It's a lot of fun," Watt added during the interview. "You have to be tough to play hockey. You have to work hard and I think that's why I was drawn to it."

He would give up his skates at the age of 13, just when he was starting to grow bigger. Another reason why he gave up playing hockey was because there were a lot of things on his plate when planning for hockey games every week. This included practices and the number of times when he would lose hockey equipment and have to get it replaced. The cost of skates can reach up to $200 for a pair easily, with quality hockey sticks costing almost as much money. Then you have your pads and helmet to go accompany that.

When you add that up between J.J. and his two younger brothers, it can cost a lot of money for a middle-class parent that probably had to scrape to afford all of that hockey equipment. Hockey would still remain a passion for Watt, who used to play center during his younger days.

Football would become the younger Watt's biggest passion when he was in the fifth grade while the family was living in Pewaukee. However, throughout his college and professional careers, Watt would always follow hockey and stated in that NHL.com interview that he hoped to attend Olympic competition sometime in the future.

In grade school, Watt was dedicated to the local football scene and even back then, he thought the quarterback for Pewaukee High School was one of the greatest players to have ever lived – even more so than Brett Favre, who at the time was setting records with the Green Bay Packers. Watt also grew up wanting to eventually become a Wisconsin Badger and to eventually join the ranks of the National Football League.

Watt said in the previously mentioned Houston Chronicle interview that he was told by one of his teachers that he could accomplish all of those dreams, as long as he was willing to put in the hard work, an aspect about Watt that could never be questioned, and who is currently playing on Sundays. Although there were a lot of people back then who had their doubts. How could anyone from such a small town in southeastern Wisconsin be able to achieve such lofty goals – while his teacher, Mrs. Keefe, was somewhat of an anomaly among the rest of the town.

"I learned quickly that people – people don't take dreams like that seriously," Watt told the Houston Chronicle in 2012.

Watt started out as a very scrawny child, but it didn't take long for him to start developing the size and muscles that came from his father's side of the family. It probably helped that his dad was also active and helped train his oldest son, as well as his two younger brothers who looked up to J.J.

Chapter 2: High School Years

Watt started off his high school football career as the backup quarterback for Pewaukee High School. It would be hard to make someone who couldn't even throw a simple bubble screen pass to lead the Pirates' offense. Watt would be introduced to the position that would best suit him – defensive end. Now, this position change didn't happen until Watt was a junior at Pewaukee, which was after Clay Iverson was named the new head coach for the Pirates. He was quite the youngster in the coaching world at the age of 27 years old.

He was also training for a period of time through a local training facility to help Watt build more into his body when he was originally only 209 pounds while standing at six-foot-five. That weight continued to increase and by the time Watt was a senior, he was weighing in at about 220 pounds.

During his four years, Watt would earn letters in football, basketball, baseball and track and field. With the Pirates football team, he would break out in his senior season as the winner of the Woodland Conference Player of the Year to highlight a season where he would earn a first-team spot on All-Conference, All-Area and All-County for both defensive end and tight end. He would also be a first-team defensive end throughout the entire state while getting an honorable mention as one of the state's best tight ends after having 26 catches for 399 receiving yards and five touchdowns to help the Pirates go 6-4 and a 6-2 record in the Woodland Conference before a loss in the district playoffs.

It's interesting that Watt wasn't being recruited as a defensive back out of high school because he had plenty of impressive stats on that side of the ball. During his senior season at Pewaukee after finishing the year with 44 and a half tackles for a loss, he was credited with 18 quarterback sacks to also receive All-

State honors as a defensive end and won the team's award for defensive Most Valuable Player. Even though he was only about 220 pounds as a six-foot-five senior, which is undersized for anyone wanting to play on the defensive line in college, his high school tape showed that he was able to make the right technical moves to get past offensive linemen to get pressure on the quarterback. Yet, the size difference was probably what kept Watt from getting offers to be a defensive end.

In addition to his football abilities, Watt was also a standout on the basketball court as someone who could score points in the paint and rebound on defense to help the Pewaukee Pirates finish with a record of 17-7 that was good enough to enter the WIAA Division II boys' basketball playoffs. Watt was also a star for the high school's track and field team as he would qualify for the Wisconsin Interscholastic Activities Association's Division II state championship in 2007 where he would set a school record in shot put with a throw of 18.25 meters (which equates to 59 feet and 11-and-a-half inches).

Yet football was the sport that he felt mot destined to play and he would consider his options of where to play college football. It was no surprise that the University of Wisconsin was on that list. The one thing that was working in Watt's favor was that he had a high school reel that was sent to college recruiters where he looked as if no one in the state of Wisconsin could stop him from getting by and causing pressure on the quarterback, if not making some form of legal contact in either a sack or tackle. However, the high school football scouting websites were not too kind to J.J. Watt. His scouting grade by the staff at ESPN.com gave him a score of 63 and ranked him as about the 172nd rated defensive end in the nation. Their analysts wrote about how he only showed his ability to make defensive plays in flashes and didn't provide the consistency of some of the top names on the list like Chicago's Martez Wilson who went to the University of Illinois. By the way, Wilson never made it to a 53-man roster in the NFL and currently plays for the Toronto Argonauts in the Canadian Football League.

He was recruited by the Badgers tight ends coordinator Bob Bostad in the fall and winter months of 2006. No offer came from the Badgers, but there was an offer from the University of Minnesota, a Big Ten rival of Wisconsin. Watt would also receive offers from Wyoming, Northern Illinois, Colorado and Central Michigan. He would choose to go with the Central Michigan Chippewas who played in the Mid-American Conference.

He might have had a better chance if it wasn't for the fact that he only had a two-star rating and was not getting a lot of quality looks from any scouts willing to make a visit to Pewaukee, Wisconsin. While he was going to go play in Mount Pleasant, Michigan, it would only be a small pit stop on Watt's road to playing in Madison. Camp Randall Stadium was the place where he dreamed of wearing red and white in front of 80,000 fans.

Chapter 3: College Years at Central Michigan, Wisconsin

Watt was not a premier receiving tight end when he played for the Central Michigan Chippewas during the 2007 season. They were a good team that finished 8-6 with a 6-1 record on route to winning the Mid-American Conference championship game. They were led by one of the better, yet more underrated, quarterbacks in the country who had completed 65.4 percent of his passes for 3,652 yards and 27 touchdowns. While most of the attention was going to either Bryan Anderson (1,132 yards, 10 touchdowns) and Antonio Brown (1,003 yards, six touchdowns), who would become a star receiver with the Pittsburgh Steelers, Watt was barely getting any catches. He had his first catch against the Ball State Cardinals on October 6, 2007, and his second catch a week later in the Chippewas win on October 13, 2007 – both for nine yards each. He had a 14-yard reception in the team's 70-14 loss at Clemson in South Carolina, followed by getting season highs with two catches and 23 yards in the team's 41-32 win over the Kent State Golden Flashes. The coaching staff at Central Michigan were talking to Watt about making a move to the offensive line. However, he felt that the move was not going to provide the opportunity to evolve very far.

After a year at Central Michigan, Watt decided to leave the school because he wanted to become a walk-on player at Wisconsin. He had spent a year taking community college courses while developing his body even more for a chance to return to football as a defensive back. He would start to get closer to the 290-pound mark that was considered a good size for somebody that was almost six and a half feet tall, but also for the position, as he was combining speed, strength, and quickness to become a better-rounded player.

His parents would eventually be willing to pay for Watt's first year of study at Wisconsin with the condition that Watt was going to attempt to earn a scholarship. Watt felt it was a tough risk, so the very least he could do was make money himself by working at a Pizza Hut while he was back in Pewaukee. The money he earned during that time was not only to help pay for his studies and textbook materials, but also for a scooter that would eventually help him get around campus. While it felt like a tough task for someone to take college courses while working as a delivery driver for the local Pizza Hut and also training on a full-time schedule. Watt would admit that it was a tough task and in many ways, it felt like he was working overtime on top of a nine-to-five job every day. Yet, it was a good feeling, because Watt knew that everything he was putting in was eventually going to pay off when he arrived on the Wisconsin campus, about 60 miles away from his hometown, while studying during the spring semester in 2008.

One of the biggest moments of Watt's career was one that he discussed in the 2012 Houston Chronicle article. He was delivering pizza to a home where a boy lived who was probably seven or eight years old at the time. He asked why the former football star from the Pewaukee Pirates was bringing him a pizza instead of in a uniform knocking people around like he did a few years ago in the red and black of the local town's football team. Watt admitted that it hurt that he had let a little kid down, one who looked up to him, and it was at that point that he vowed he was going to turn things around and be the football star the young boy looked at him as. Maybe he wasn't going to necessarily become the next great NFL legend, but Watt wanted to at least achieve some form of greatness and be a positive role model once again.

Eventually, Watt would become a walk-on at Wisconsin and was redshirted during the 2008 season. It was at that point that Watt was able to say that he had proven that it was possible. He was receiving an opportunity to play for the college team that he had dreamed to be a part of throughout his childhood. Because of that, Watt would put in even more hours of study in the classroom, in film sessions with the team, and in the weight room, as he would hope to be one of the great contributors to a Badgers team that had suffered a bit of a down year in 2008 with a 7-6 record that concluded with a 42-13 loss to Florida State in the Champ Sports Bowl. It was a fall after head coach Bret Bielema's first season in 2006 that was a 12-1 season and winning the Capital One Bowl over Arkansas, 17-14.

While Watt was a redshirt for the 2008 season (which is when a school will have a player on the team, but will not have him in any games, which saves a year of eligibility) and was a very valuable component for Wisconsin's scout team. That's because he was coming in at an amazing level of fitness and was able to bench press well above the 400-pound mark, which is a great sign of how strong of a player he was. It would be a dream for any college football coach to have a new player who has that kind of strength before being able to help him develop further. It was because of the early days of practice where the coaching staff confirmed that Watt would be a better fit in making the transition of being a tight end on offense to becoming a defensive end.

While scout teams are usually composed of redshirted players and those who are not able to make the main roster, they help simulate what the team will be facing by mimicking the plays that the Badgers would expect to deal with in their upcoming games. By the end of the season, Watt was considered Wisconsin's Scout Player of the Year thanks to weekly honors for his efforts in the practices leading up to the Badgers' contests against Akron on August 30, 2008 (38-17 win); at Iowa on October 18, 2008 (38-16 loss); and when they hosted the Minnesota Gophers on November 15, 2008 (35-32 win).

Even though he wasn't making the main Badgers roster who played on Saturdays, Watt was still invited to watch film in the office of defensive coordinator Charlie Patridge after dinner every night. During an interview with *ESPN – The Magazine's* Elizabeth Merrill, Watt explained that he kept himself motivated to remain dedicated, which wasn't easy all the time. In fact, he admitted to having some thoughts of other things he could be doing with his time rather than sitting and watching film by himself in a coach's office. All he would have to do though was turn around and look out the window towards Camp Randall Stadium where he was always picturing himself making plays on defense every game day, similar to how he did back at high school in Pewaukee. In the meantime, he was also maintaining a strict diet to optimize his muscle growth during this season of development on the practice squad – six meals per day that featured chicken and vegetables as primary components, as well as protein shakes at the end of the day and after workouts. He was finally able to make his debut with the Badgers at the beginning of the 2009 season with his proud family sitting amongst the more than 80,000 fans in the early September season opener.

The 2009 season started well for the Badgers with a win over the Mid-American Conference's Northern Illinois Huskies with a score of 28-20 on September 5, 2009. In the season-opening contest at Camp Randall Stadium, Watt would finish with three solo tackles and three assisted tackles, along with a half-tackle for a loss and a half-sack. Watt also deflected one pass while playing the weak side defensive end. It would take some getting used to, but Watt was progressive in becoming a better part part of a strong defensive line for the Badgers, getting two tackles in the team's 34-31 double-overtime win at home against the Fresno State Bulldogs. Watt would not play in the Badgers win on September 19, 2009, against Wofford, but he would return in time for the start of Big Ten Conference and play to get one tackle for a loss in the

Badgers' 38-30 win over the Michigan State Spartans on September 26, 2009. Following that performance, Watt would collect another four total tackles, two for a loss, in the team's 31-28 victory at Minnesota on October 3, 2009, in the annual Battle for Paul Bunyan's Axe.

The team was looking good, but Wisconsin would then be pitted against the two top teams in the Big Ten in the Ohio State Buckeyes (finishing 11-2 and fifth-ranked in the country) and the Iowa Hawkeyes (finishing 11-2 and seventh-ranked in the country). Wisconsin would suffer their first loss of the season by falling to the Buckeyes in Columbus, Ohio, in a 31-13 loss on October 10, 2009. Despite the Badgers only allowing 184 yards of offense to Ohio State, the Badgers' quarterback Scott Tolzien would throw two interceptions that were returned for touchdowns. Watt himself would complete three tackles in the losing effort. One week later, Watt had his best game of the season with eight tackles (seven of which were solo) with four tackles for a loss and one sack on October 17, 2009 in a 20-10 loss to Iowa.

After a bye week, the Badgers would bounce back from the back-to-back losses starting with a 37-0 shutout win over the Purdue Boilermakers on October 31, 2009 at home. Watt would collect another three tackles (two solo) with one tackle for loss and a deflected pass. He would get another three tackles in each of the Badgers wins on November 7, 2009, with a 31-28 win in Bloomington, Indiana, and again on November 14, 2009, in a 45-24 win back at Camp Randall Stadium against the Michigan Wolverines. As the team was climbing back into the top 25 rankings with to the 17th spot in the polls, the Badgers would suffer to an upset in Evanston, Illinois, with a 33-31 loss on November 21, 2009, where Watt have just two solo tackles against the Wildcats.

The Badgers would get a chance to close out the regular season with a victory on the road to face the

Hawaii Rainbow Warriors in a lopsided 51-10 victory on December 5, 2009, where Watt had six solo tackles, three of them for a loss, with a season-high of two sacks in the win. It would be several weeks before the Badgers would be back on the football field as the 24th-ranked team in the nation and facing the 14th-ranked Miami (FL) Hurricanes in the Champs Sports Bowl in Orlando, Florida, on December 29, 2009. While it was a close win on the scoreboard for the Badgers at 20-14, the Wisconsin defense held the Hurricanes to only 249 total offensive yards, only 61 of which came from running the ball. Watt would finish with three tackles, two for a loss and one sack while also deflecting two passes from the line.

It was a good ending to the season as the Badgers would finish with a 10-3 overall record and finished with a final ranking as the 16th team in the nation, according to the Associated Press poll. It was a great year after a few disappointing seasons. Watt ended his first year with the Badgers as a redshirt sophomore with 44 total tackles, 32 of which were solo and 15 and a half for a loss to go along with five defended passes and four-and-a-half sacks. He also had two fumbled recoveries on the season. Watt was making himself known on defense while earning his first varsity letter with the Badgers in that season.

In the 2010 season, Watt and the Wisconsin defense would take bigger strides in becoming one of the nation's best. In the Badgers first game on September 4, 2010, Watt had four total tackles (two solo, two assisted) and forced one fumble during the team's season-opener at the University of Nevada-Las Vegas (better known as UNLV), a 41-21 win where the Rebels could only finish with about 217 total yards. Watt also deflected three passes while playing on the defensive line for a well-rounded game. In the Badgers' home opening 27-14 win over San Jose State on September 11, 2010, Watt would finish with six tackles, four solo and two-and-a-half for a loss, against the Spartans. He would struggle in the final two games of Wisconsin's with a total of four tackles between the Badgers' wins on September 18, 2010, against Arizona State (20-19) September 25, 2010, and against Austin Peay (70-3).

Watt's best game while at Wisconsin would come during their Big Ten Conference opening game on October 2, 2010. Despite the 34-24 loss at Michigan State, he would have 10 total tackles with two-and-a-half for a loss while also adding one quarterback sack and a couple of pass deflections. It would be the lone conference loss for the Badgers as they bounced back in a 41-23 win over the Minnesota Gophers on October 9, 2010, where Watt had six tackles, one tackle for a loss and one quarterback sack. In their next game at home against the Ohio State Buckeyes, Watt would get another four solo tackles (three of them for a loss) and another two sacks as the Badgers upset the then top-ranked team in the nation with a 31-18 win at Camp Randall Stadium.

The Badgers would have to follow that up with another tough matchup on the road against the then 13th-ranked Iowa Hawkeyes October 23, 2010, at Kinnick Stadium in Iowa City, Iowa. Watt had another big day with five total tackles, two for a loss, and one sack as the Badgers would squeak out a 31-30 win. Watt would get another four tackles and one sack in the team's 34-13 win at Purdue University on November 6, 2010, followed by another three tackles in a blowout win at home over the Indiana Hoosiers by a score of 83-20 as the offense totaled just a few yards short of the 600-mark.

Watt would also get a first during the Badgers' road game in Ann Arbor, Michigan on November 20, 2010, against the Michigan Wolverines. During the 48-28 win, Watt would get his first interception on his second defended pass and returned 15 yards to go along with six total tackles (four solo and two assisted). The momentum continued for Watt as he would get seven solo tackles, three for a loss, one quarterback sack and two forced fumbles (two of the team's seven created turnovers) in a 70-23 win at home against the Northwestern Wildcats.

After completing their regular season schedule, the Badgers were 11-1 (7-1 in the Big Ten) and had a share of the Big Ten Conference championship with Michigan State and Ohio State – although the Buckeyes would later vacate all 12 of their wins that season, including their Sugar Bowl victory over Arkansas, and their share of the conference championship. In addition to helping the Badgers have the share of the conference championship and help the team reach the No. 3 ranking in the polls, Watt earned some hardware himself after finishing the season with 59 tackles, 21 for loss, sacking opposing quarterbacks seven times, recovery two fumbles and one interception.

With those impressive numbers for the defensive end, Watt named the winner of the 2010 Ronnie Lott

Impact Trophy that was given to the impact defensive player of the year. Watt joined a list of winners that included David Pollack out of Georgia, Glenn Dorsey out of Louisiana State (also known as LSU) and James Laurinaitis from Ohio State. Watt would also be named a second-team All-American athlete by the Associated Press and Sports Illustrated magazine while also receiving first-team conference honors both for his athletic abilities and his studies in the classroom, majoring in life sciences communication. Above all of that, Watt was named Wisconsin's Most Valuable Player. Not bad for that once scrawny and tall kid out of Pewaukee, Wisconsin, about 60 miles from where he was playing in front of 80,000 in proud red and white Badger attire.

Wisconsin would earn the Big Ten's selection to play in the Rose Bowl on January 1, 2011, to face an undefeated Texas Christian University, who were considered a Cinderella of sorts by going undefeated and breaking into the Bowl Championship Series by finishing the regular season with a No. 4 ranking in the computer polls to set up a very high quality game against the Badgers (who were No. 3) in Pasadena, California. It was a close game where both teams played pretty evenly with no turnovers and with both having around 300 total offensive yards. However, TCU quarterback Andy Dalton would be the leader for the Horned Frogs with 219 yards, one passing touchdown and another one ran in to help give TCU the upset win to complete the perfect season – albeit without a National Championship – by defeating Wisconsin 21-19 at the Rose Bowl. Watt finished with three total tackles, but couldn't get anything done in the backfield in terms of tackles for loss or sacks.

It was a great season for Watt and despite the Wisconsin fans showing excitement to see what he would do for his senior season with the Badgers, Watt decided that he would forgo his senior year at Wisconsin and would be entered into the 2011 NFL Draft. He stated in a goodbye announcement in a press conference that he loved every minute of being with the Wisconsin Badgers – from the football to watching basketball to his classes and even the city of Madison.

Watt had accomplished his dream of being a star player for the University of Wisconsin, and now he had his sights set on his next target of becoming a star player for one of the 32 teams in the NFL.

Chapter 4: Watt's NFL Career

After making the decision to jump to the NFL, the first step of being able to play on Sundays was going through the Rookie Combine that was held in February 2011 at Lucas Oil Stadium in Indianapolis, Indiana. This was considered the best time to make a major impact on how you were judged by the NFL scouts from all 32 teams in the league. Watt was able to do that as he came in as his six-foot-five, 290-pound physique that was easily noticed. He wasn't the fastest in the 40-yard dash, but it wasn't too far from the leaders at about 4.81 seconds –which is still a good mark for someone of his size. He was also able to do a 10-yard split in about 1.64 seconds, the 20-yard split in 2.71 seconds and completed the three-cone agility drill in just under seven seconds. He was also a standout for his strength with a total of 34 repetitions of bench pressing the 225-pound weight given to all Combine participants. In addition to his opportunities to show his speed and strength, he was also able to complete the vertical jump at about 37 inches and then performed a 10-foot broad jump.

Now in addition to his physical skills, Watt also scored a 31 on the Wonderlic Cognitive Ability Test, which is famously used by NFL teams to see how well the new batch of rookies can show their aptitude for solving problems that could translate to being able to think quickly on the field when faced with a variety of adversities to find success. The average player in the NFL would score about 20 on this Wonderlic test, while a perfect score would be 50. Watt's 31 was close to players like Green Bay quarterback Aaron Rodgers' 35 and a lot better than other notable players who have had scores as low as 4 (i.e. Morris Claiborne from the 2012 NFL Draft).

Yet with all of those statistics from the NFL Combine, Watt was marked with a grade of 8.37 out of 10, which fell within the range that predicts whether or not a player will be capable of becoming an All-Pro player in the league. The experts from the NFL were considering Watt as a perfect fit for a team that uses a 4-3 defensive scheme – four linemen and three linebackers. However, experts speculated that there might be some benefits to using him as an end in a 3-4 – three linemen and four linebackers. He did receive some negative marks for not being considered a fast start off the line and attacking blocks, but made up for it with his ability pursue the quarterback with straight-line speed. When you add a motor that doesn't want to stop at all to a high football mentality, there were many who thought that Watt was going to be a future defensive NFL MVP.

There were some negative marks on Watt's overall analysis that was posted on the combine database found on NFL.com. Watt was considered a defensive end that wasn't going to get the edge on the offensive tackles on a consistent basis and there were some critiques about how he couldn't come off the line with enough quickness to be effective on the pass rush or to stop the run. They were also saying that while he was someone who could fight to hold his own ground, he struggled with the double team while the NFL.com staff experts felt he didn't have enough lateral mobility and could struggle with keeping a quarterback or running back contained between the tackles.

Moving on to the NFL Draft held at Radio City Music Hall in New York City, New York on April 28, 2011, there were a number of players who were waiting in the back for their name to be called to come up on stage in the first round. Watt was one of 56 underclassmen who would leave college football with at least one year of eligibility remaining; this was a record compared to other NFL Draft classes. There was a lot of talent that NFL teams had to consider with Cam Newton, who had won the 2010 Heisman Trophy with the Auburn Tigers, going first overall to the Carolina Panthers. The second selection was Texas A&M linebacker Von Miller going to Denver, followed by Alabama defensive end Marcell Dareus going third to the Buffalo Bills.

As the selections were made, there were a number of Houston Texans fans that were not completely happy with J.J. Watt being picked as the 11th overall selection. That is because many Houston faithful were wanting the team to select Nick Fairley, a defensive lineman coming out of Auburn, or even Prince Amukamara, a cornerback from Nebraska. However, one thing that everyone should know about people with a higher motor and a high work drive like Watt, adding more motivation to prove his upset fans wrong was only a positive. While there were doubters among the fan base, Texans head Coach Wade Philips was confident in Watt being successful. So was the team overall as they immediately signed him to a four-year contract worth $11.24 million just before start of Houston's training camp.

In the 2011 season-opener against AFC South Divisional rival Indianapolis on September 11, 2011, Watt had made an immediate impact with five tackles and even recovered a fumble late in the first quarter as the Texans held the Colts to only 236 offensive yards in a 34-7 victory. Watt would collect another three tackles in a close win on the road in Miami on September 18, 2011 in a 23-13 win. It would be the Texans third game where Watt would record his first sack on New Orleans Saints quarterback Drew Brees to go along with four tackles in a losing effort, 40-33 on September 25, 2011, in the Louisiana Superdome. These were good games, but Watt would be somewhat ineffective in terms of tackles with just one in the October 2, 2011, win (17-10) over the Pittsburgh Steelers and on October 9, 2011, (25-20 loss) against the Oakland Raiders.

However, Watt would bounce back with three tackles and one sack in the team's 41-7 win on October 23, 2011, in Tennessee in one of the team's more dominant defensive performances. Titans quarterback Matt Hasselbeck was 14 out of 30 for 104 yards and two interceptions while the running backs only had 53 yards on the ground game. That win was the start of a very long winning streak to help Houston try to earn their first playoff berth. That momentum continued for Watt with five tackles in a Texans 24-14 win at home against division rival Jacksonville Jaguars on October 30, 2011. On November 6, 2011, while Watt only had two tackles against the Cleveland Browns, he would recover a fumble forced by teammate DeMeco Ryans in a 30-12 win at home over the Browns. This was followed by having three tackles and a half sack in a 37-9 win over the Tampa Bay Buccaneers on November 13, 2011.

One of Watt's best individual performances in his rookie season was on November 27, 2011, where he would get two sacks in addition to five tackles to help the Texans defeat the Jaguars in Jacksonville, 20-13. It was a great game, but Watt would have a game that was a polar opposite on December 4, 2011, where he had no tackles, sacks, or anything else on his statistical line, while Houston would defeat the Atlanta Falcons, 17-10. He would bounce back with three tackles in a 20-19 win over the Cincinnati Bengals on December 11, 2011. The Texans were looking good with a 10-3 record and had a seven-game winning streak despite having had to use three different starting quarterbacks thanks to a number of injuries and other issues – Matt Schaub, Matt Leinart and T.J. Yates.

However, offensive issues would catch up to the Texans down the stretch as they would lose their final three games of the season. Watt would do well with five tackles in the team's 28-13 loss to the Carolina Panthers on December 18, 2011, followed by another five tackles and a sack in a 19-16 loss on the road to the Indianapolis Colts. They would get only one tackle in the team's loss to the Tennessee Titans on New Year's Day – January 1, 2012 – in a 23-22 close decision.

While it was a tough losing streak to end the 2011-12 NFL season, the Texans were able to win the AFC South Division with a 10-6 record with a one-game lead over the Titans (9-7) to earn the automatic playoff berth. Watt would finish the regular season of his rookie season having started in all 16 games and finishing with 49 tackles, 5 and a half sacks and having defended 4 passes for a season that made him the Texans Rookie of the Year. Additional honors included being named to the U.S.A. Today's All-Joe squad and also being picked for the All-Rookie teams composed by Pro-Football Weekly and the Pro Football Writers of America.

Having helped the Houston Texans clinch their first playoff spot since becoming an expansion franchise that started in the 2002 season, Watt was looking forward to playing in the AFC Wildcard round in a rematch of the Rose Bowl loss he suffered with the Wisconsin Badgers a little more than a year before; that's because the TCU Horned Frogs quarterback

Andy Dalton was now leading the Cincinnati Bengals. On January 7, 2012, the Texans helped Watt exact some revenge against Dalton with a 31-10 shutout. Watt was a big player in this game with two tackles and one sack. Just before the first half ended though, Watt would pick one of Dalton's three interceptions and returned it 29 yards for a touchdown to break a 10-10 tie for a lead that the Texans would not relinquish for the rest of the game.

However, the Texans first playoff appearance would fall short of advancing to the AFC Championship game as the Texans fell to the Baltimore Ravens, 20-13, at M&T Bank Stadium in Baltimore, Maryland on January 15, 2012. Watt had put up numbers that surpassed much of what he did during his rookie season with 9 total tackles and had 2 sacks. He earned a half credit on another to make Joe Flacco's job a little tougher, although he was able to compile a 17-3 lead in the first quarter that the Texans attempted to come back from. The Ravens were a good team, but were defeated by the New England Patriots who would drop the Super Bowl to the New York Giants. Overall, the Houston fans were happy with the fact their team made the playoffs and believed that they were seeing the start of something special, including the player they booed when he was initially announced nearly a year before at the 2011 NFL Draft.

The 2012 NFL season would prove to be a breakout season for Watt, although it had a quiet start on September 9, 2012, in a 30-10 win over the Miami Dolphins after collecting two tackles and a half credit for a quarterback sack with Antonio Smith. It was clear that quiet start wouldn't last very long when Watt collected four tackles, one and a half sacks, and recovered a fumble to help Houston get an AFC South win, 27-7, in Jacksonville on September 16, 2012.

There would be an early season test for the Texans as they faced a revamped Denver Broncos team on September 25, 2012, which featured Peyton Manning, who was hoping to return from being out for an entire season and was released by the Indianapolis Colts. Watt was a bother for Manning with two and a half sacks, along with six tackles to help Houston stay ahead of the Broncos at Sports Authority Field at Mile High, 31-25. Watt would continue to add to his sack totals with another two on Matt Hasselbeck in the team's 38-14 victory at home against the Tennessee Titans on September 30, 2012. Watt also had four tackles and recovered a fumble forced by teammate Antonio Smith.

On October 8, 2012, the Texans would extend the team's undefeated streak with a 23-17 win over the New York Jets where Watt would get four tackles and one sack. It was also a game where Watt would deflect three of Jets quarterback Mark Sanchez's passes that affected him enough to throw two interceptions in the game. Pass deflections were somewhat of a big part of his sophomore season with the Houston Texans having 10 passes defended in his first seven games, which earned him the nickname "J.J. Swatt," which came to a surprise to some NFL experts even though he was able to defend passes pretty well from the line while playing for the Wisconsin Badgers. The winning streak would end at home on October 14, 2012, to the Green Bay Packers, 42-24, despite Watt having five tackles and two sacks.

Watt would have some struggles on October 21, 2012, in a 43-13 win over the Baltimore Ravens where he had two tackles. After a bye week, Watt returned to form to collect another four tackles and a sack in the team's 21-9 win over the Buffalo Bills on November 4, 2012, followed by another two tackles in Houston's 13-6 win visiting the Chicago Bears on November 11, 2012. The former Badger would continue to rack up record numbers with another 8 total tackles (6 solo, 2 assisted) and 1 sack to help the Texans defeat the Jaguars at home in a 43-37 win on November 18, 2012. That was quickly followed up with another five tackles and three sacks on the road in a close 34-31 road win visiting the Detroit Lions on November 22, 2012, which was an overtime game that was decided by costly mistakes including a missed field goal from Detroit kicker Jason Hanson and an unsportsmanlike conduct penalty on head coach Jim Schwartz.

The numbers would continue to grow for Watt, who would get another two-sack game on the road on December 2, 2012 in a key road victory at Tennessee, 24-10. At this point in the season, the Texans were looking like the favorite to win the top overall playoff season in the AFC. They had virtually locked their second consecutive playoff appearance for just as many times in franchise history at a 12-1 record. Unfortunately, the team would lose three of their next four games on November 10, 2012 against the New England Patriots (42-14); on November 23, 2012, against the Minnesota Vikings (23-6); and on November 30, 2012, against the Indianapolis Colts on the road (28-16). During those three losses, Watt would total 11 tackles with 1 sack and 1 defended pass.

One highlight late in the season featured the first time in Watt's young NFL career that he would have at least 10 tackles in a single game in a win over the Colts in Houston on November 16, 2012, by a score of 29-17. Watt also had three sacks on Colts' quarterback Andrew Luck. By the end of the regular season, the Houston Texans were still at the top of the AFC South with a record of 12-4. They had fallen out of the top overall spot due to those three out of four losses to end the regular season, which allowed the Denver Broncos to take first overall in the conference with a 13-3 record, followed by the New England Patriots with a 12-4 records (they held the tiebreaker from beating Houston back on December 10, 2012).

For Watt, he would finish the season having started all 16 games at defensive end and had career highs 69 solo tackles, another 12 assisted tackles, and led the

NFL with 20 and a half sacks on the season – unreal numbers to put together one of the best in the league's history. He broke the team's sack record, which was once held by Mario Williams with 14.5 sacks. It's no surprise that he was named the Texans MVP, but he received almost all of the votes to be named the NFL's Defensive Player of the Year Award (49 out of 50 votes). Watt was the first Houston Texans player in team history to win this award and only the 17th defensive linemen and eighth defensive end in history to do so. The praise didn't stop there as he would receive a number of accolades from the NFL, not only for his dominant play, but for how he was technically sound in doing so. Watt received the AFC Defensive Player of the Year from NFL 101 and was also named to USA Football's Fundamentals Team.

The success continued as Watt was part of some big plays in the Texans' 19-13 win over the Cincinnati Bengals on January 5, 2013, during the AFC Wildcard Playoffs. Watt had 1 sack on Andy Dalton to go along with 5 tackles and deflecting 2 passes. They would find themselves back in Foxboro, Massachusetts in a game against the high-powered offense in the New England Patriots on January 13, 2013. The Patriots would win 41-28, as Watt was only able to get one solo tackle, three assisted and just a partial credit on a Tom Brady sack. The Patriots would lose the AFC Championship to the Baltimore Ravens, who would move on to defeat the San Francisco 49ers in Super Bowl XLVII. Watt would be selected to his first Pro Bowl in 2012, but would not play in the actual game where the AFC defeated the NFC on January 30, 2013, in Honolulu, Hawaii. The score was 59-41 for the red team.

There was a lot of hope leading up to the 2013 season and there were some high expectations. With a combination of poor quarterback play from Matt Schaub, including a number of interceptions returned for touchdowns and an inconsistency in offense, the Texans would finish with only a 2-14 record and near the bottom of the league's overall standings. However, Watt would still have a very productive season. Once again, he started in all 16 of the regular season games and finished 6 solo tackles, another 15 assisted, and about 10 and a half sacks. Additionally, he would deflect seven passes and force four fumbles as he maintained his dominance in the AFC, despite the Texans losing record.

The season did start off well for the Texans with a 2-0 beginning thanks to a 31-28 victory on the road against the San Diego Chargers on September 9, 2013, where Watt would get two solo tackles, one assisted and a deflected pass. He had more success against the Tennessee Titans in the home opener on September 15, 2013, with two sacks on Titans' quarterback Jake Locker to go along with five solo tackles and another pass deflection to help the Texans win 30-24. The Texans would suffer their first loss of the season on the road on September 22, 2013, in a 30-9 decision to the Baltimore Ravens, a game where Watt had nine total tackles (six solo, three assisted) with one sack of Joe Flacco.

The streak continued during a home game against the Seattle Seahawks on September 29, 2013, which was at the time considered to be an early preview of a potential Super Bowl at the end of the 2013-2014 season. Watt would play a decent game individually with eight total tackles and a partial sack, but Houston's Schaub threw two interceptions that included one by Seattle cornerback Richard Sherman returning it 58 yards for the score to tie the game 20-20 at regulation, and the Seahawks would win in overtime, 23-20, with a 45-yard field goal from Steven Hauschka.

While the Texans would lose the rest of their games that season, Watt would still put up dependable numbers on defense, including a performance on November 17, 2013 in the 28-23 loss to the Oakland Raiders where Watt had five solo tackles and two quarterback sacks. That game was followed up with nine tackles and one sack in the home loss to the Jacksonville Jaguars, 13-6, on November 24, 2013. He would reach the nine tackle mark one more time in the season-concluding 16-10 loss on December 29, 2013, at Tennessee with all nine tackles solo and one sack.

As disappointing as the season was for Houston, Watt was still given a lot of praise for what he did on his own performance. Watt still received a nomination to the NFL's first team All-Pro squad for the second consecutive season, along with being named to the AFC Pro Bowl for the second time in as many years. This was also a new format for the NFL's annual Pro Bowl game where instead of having All-Star teams represent each conference, the teams were drafted by coaches Jerry Rice and Deion Sanders. Watt was on Team Sanders and had one sack and two deflected passes with Team Rice winning 22-21 on January 26, 2014, at Aloha Stadium in Honolulu, Hawaii.

However, there were some big changes made as Gary Kubiak was fired by the Houston Texans after he had developed a playoff contender after taking over for Dom Capers to be the team's second coach ever. The team felt that they were capable of a lot more, at least better than the 2-11 stretch the led to Kubiak being released in the middle of the season. Wade Phillips, who was a former head coach of the Dallas Cowboys, took over on an interim basis for the last three games of the season. The 2-14 record after the 12-4 playoff season in 2012 tied an NFL record for biggest decline in total wins between seasons. The 1993 Houston Oilers had 12 wins before winning only two in 1994. It was no surprise when the Texans owner Robert McNair stated after the season that they just wanted to "kick 2013 the hell out of the door." It would be a few days later when they named a new head coach, Bill O'Brien.

If O'Brien had anything on his list worth making him the next Texans head coach, it was the fact that he took over the Penn State University football program in the aftermath of long-time head coach Joe Paterno being let go in the middle of the Jerry Sandusky child sex abuse scandal. Right away, he helped the Nittany Lions go 8-4 and he would be considered the Coach of the Year in 2012. Therefore, it wasn't long before he was getting interest from other NFL teams like the Philadelphia Eagles and the Cleveland Browns. After another season, he felt that he couldn't say no any longer and accepted the offer to come to Houston. Most of his work was on the offensive side of the ball, having served as a wide receiver and quarterback coach between 2008 and 2010 for the New England Patriots before serving as the offensive coordinator in 2011.

The Texans remained extremely busy leading up to the 2014 season and decided they wanted to reward Watt for having played very well during his first three seasons in the NFL. Therefore, the Texans offered Watt a six-year contract extension worth $100 million.

This featured a first year salary of $30.9 million and a clause for an additional $21 million if he is on the roster at the beginning of 2016. Houston was showing that they were willing to invest in Watt by making him the highest paid player in the NFL that doesn't play in the quarterback position. Watt was investing himself into not only being a better football player, but to helping the Texans to become a better team. One thing was for sure, Watt was going to get to a good start of what would be a memorable season in 2014 in his fourth year in the NFL

The Texans won their first game of the season at home on September 7, 2014, by beating the Washington Redskins, 17-6. Watt had three total tackles (two solo and one assisted) with his first sack of the season. Nothing really out of the ordinary for one of the league's best defensive players. He was about to accomplish a number of firsts in 2014, starting with his first ever touchdown catch. On September 14, 2014 against the Oakland Raiders, Watt lined up as a tight end and caught a one-yard pass from Houston quarterback Ryan Fitzpatrick in the first quarter of a 30-14 win on the road. It was the first time any defensive player from the Texans would score a touchdown on an offensive play, but Watt wasn't like most players after having years of high school and collegiate experience playing on offense as well.

While Watt would continue to play well defensively with a seven-tackle and one sack performance in the Texans' 30-17 loss to the New York Giants on September 21, 2014, he would score another touchdown the following week, this time on defense. On September 28, 2014, in a home game against the Buffalo Bills, Watt would intercept Bills' quarterback E.J. Manual and returned the ball 80 yards for a "pick-six" touchdown early in the third quarter to help Houston get a key 23-17 win. It was the fourth longest interception return in Texans history and also the sixth longest return by someone on defense. In addition to the interception touchdown, Watt also had five tackles (two solo, three assisted) and also hit Manual nine times to keep the pressure on the Buffalo quarterback. The only negative thing that happened to Watt was that he was penalized twice for roughing the quarterback and was fined about $16,000 for one of those hits.

This was followed by collecting four tackles in a losing effort in Dallas by falling to the Cowboys 20-17 on October 5, 2014. He would bounce back with another game on October 9, 2014 as the big star with seven total tackles, two sacks and three deflected passes against the Indianapolis Colts in a 33-28 loss. During one of his sacks with Colts quarterback Andrew Luck, Watt would return the loose ball into the endzone for a 45-yard touchdown return.

His defensive numbers would continue to grow, including his sack totals with one sack in the team's 23-20 loss in Pittsburgh on October 20, 2014, and another two sacks during the Texans' 30-16 win in Tennessee to help. Watt would have one of his better games with seven total tackles (four solo, three assisted) along with one and a half sacks in a 31-21 loss at home to the Philadelphia Eagles on November 2, 2014. While Watt was once again putting up some impressive numbers on defense (and offense), the Texans entered their bye week with a 4-5 record which, considering how bad the Texans were the prior year, was a big improvement for Houston.

In the Texans' first game back from the bye week, Watt would explode for another great game on both sides of the ball. Watt would catch a two-yard pass from quarterback Ryan Mallett (his first ever touchdown pass in his first ever career start) to start off the scoring in the first quarter on November 16, 2014. Watt also recorded five tackles, one sack, a forced fumble and a fumble recovery to help the Texans get a 23-7 win over the Cleveland Browns. Watt would follow that up with seven more tackles in the 22-13 loss to the Cincinnati Bengals on November 23, 2014. He would also get another two sacks and three tackles while also forcing one fumble in the team's big 45-21 victory over the AFC South rival Tennessee Titans – Watt also caught his third goal-line touchdown pass for one-yard from Ryan Fitzpatrick.

In the next week, Watt would have a season-high with three sacks against the Jacksonville Jaguars on December 7, 2014, to go along with four tackles while the Texans earned the road win, 27-13. This was followed up by another two sacks and six tackles in a losing effort, 17-10, to the Indianapolis Colts on December 14, 2014. All of these numbers were building up to Watt getting his 54th sack of his career on December 21, 2014, which gave him the sole lead for most sacks in Houston Texans history, surpassing Mario Williams. And after having so many firsts in the 2014 season, Watt would add another first with a sack for a safety during the team's December 28, 2014, game against the Jaguars during a 23-17 win where Watt had six solo tackles, three sacks and a forced fumble.

It was an impressive season for Watt in just about every facet possible for the defensive end. After staring all 16 games in the 2014 season, Watt finished with 78 total tackles (59 solo, 19 assisted), 20 and a half sacks (which tied his career high from 2012), four forced fumbles and one interception. In addition to his defensive numbers, Watt had a total of five touchdowns (three of them as an offensive tight end) to be the first defensive lineman in league history to have at least five touchdowns in a single season since 1944. Watt's dominance earned him a spot on as an NFL All-Pro first team player and was also named the NFL's Defensive Player of the Year for just the second time in three years and a number of other honors and awards.

For the third season in a row, Watt was selected to be in the NFL's annual Pro Bowl held January 25, 2015, at the University of Phoenix Stadium in Glendale, Ariz., where Cris Carter and Michael Irvin were the team captains. Carter selected Watt to be the captain of his defense. Watt would get one interception and recover a fumble, along with an assisted tackle, in a losing effort as Team Irwin defeated Team Carter, 32-28.

The 2015 season is currently underway as Watt has already had a fast start to another big season, which began with nine tackles and two sacks in the season opening loss, 27-20, to the Kansas City Chiefs on September 13, 2015. In the very next game on September 20, 2015, Watt would collect another five tackles (four solo, one assisted) with one sack and two deflected passes in a 24-17 loss to the Carolina Panthers.

The Texans had a slow start to the season with losses in four of their first five games, but the team has won four of the last five as of November 22, 2015. During that second set of five games, Watt has continued to add to his sack total with two sacks and seven tackles in a 44-26 loss to the Miami Dolphins on October 25,

2015, followed by another two and a half sacks with five tackles in a 20-6 win over the Tennessee Titans on November 1, 2015. His most recent performance, as of this writing, was an eight tackle game with two quarterback sacks in the Texans' 24-17 win over the New York Jets on November 22, 2015.

Even though the team is hovering around the .500 win-loss mark, there have been a number of injuries throughout the AFC South, and if the Texans can reach their 9-7 mark like the year before, there's a belief that that would be enough to win the division and earn an automatic berth into the playoffs. While Houston's offense has had some issues the past few years, a defense led by J.J. Watt could be a dangerous foe for anyone in the playoffs. Maybe not in 2015, but there could come a season down the road where Houston could be a legitimate championship contender.

Chapter 5: Watt's Personal Life

When J.J. Watt signed his first NFL contract with the Houston Texans back in 2011, he decided to buy his own home in Pearland, Texas, which is about a 30-minute commute to Houston. It was far enough from the hustle and bustle of the bigger city in Houston and provided a prairie-like setting to live in with farms that grew various fruits and vegetables. It reminded Watt of life in the small town of Pewaukee, Wisconson, which is why he decided to purchase a four-bedroom home for about $400,000, thanks to the signing bonus of his rookie contract.

Over the years, he would stay in Texas while playing in the NFL and continuing to make history as one of the league's best defensive stars. However, he likely didn't feel 100 percent at home during the offseason. So after signing one of the largest contract extensions in NFL history for a defensive linemen, he decided to purchase a new home back in his hometown in

Wisconsin that is nestled about 15 miles away from his childhood hometown of Pewaukee.

He told the Houston Chronicle that he was going to get away during the offseason with a cabin that was in the middle of nowhere so that he could live his life off the field without any distractions and, in a lot of ways, very minimally. Yet the log cabin is very spacious with a total of 4,500 square feet of living space on top of about 35 acres of land. Records show that he purchased the home for about $800,000. It is the perfect place for someone who loves to get away from the pressures that the media can sometimes place on a player, and who wouldn't want to get away from everyone during the offseason, which is meant to recoup, recover, and get prepared for the new season and the training camp in the late summer?

Back in a 2012 story with the Houston Chronicle, Watt said that Pewaukee, Wisconsin is where he wants to spend his time after playing football. The plan in his mind is that he will bring his future wife to raise their children in the community that raised and supported him into becoming the NFL star and positive role model he continues to be. You can accredit that to how he was supported in his pursuits of football and how he had so many great memories from the backyard football between his house and the yard two houses down, while also knowing how the teachers would likely be a positive influence on his future children. With a log cabin and a complete family, all he would need are a few dogs, maybe a couple of horses since he has the property to build a ranch or farm, or maybe to enjoy some other outdoor activities.

Family is also one of the most important things about Watt, which is why he actively supports his brothers who are also making quite the big names for themselves in their respective football careers. His middle brother Derek was also recruited out of Pewaukee High School after his career there, where he finished with 2,685 rushing yards and 44 touchdowns on the ground. He also had an additional 625 yards receiving with five touchdown catches. On defense, he also totaled about 140 tackles as a linebacker, 27 for a loss, five forced fumbles and three interceptions with the Pewaukee Pirates. Derek Watt would accept an offer to go to the University of Wisconsin, just like his older brother did, and was redshirted in 2011 while also being one of the team's best defensive scout team players – once again, like his older brother. Derek would play in all 14 games in the 2012 season and played several more as a fullback for the Badgers. He only had one touchdown during the Badgers' home game against the Northwestern Wildcats on October 12, 2013, only a three-yard from quarterback Joel Stave in a 35-6 win.

Derek Watt, who stands at six-foot-one and weighs about 236 pounds (the smallest of the three Watt brothers) is projected as one of the top fullbacks for the 2016 NFL Draft. Granted there are some offenses in the professional ranks who are focused more on having a passing offense that doesn't always need a fullback, Watt is projected in the later rounds of the draft with the worst case scenario of going undrafted and possibly being signed by a team as a rookie free agent.

The youngest Watt, T.J., was also another tight end who was a star for the Pewaukee Pirates in that position. In fact he was ranked 28th by ESPN and 44th nationally by Scout.com as a three-star recruit. Overall, he did play some quarterback with in his senior year with 527 yards passing with seven touchdowns, and also ran for another 554 yards and nine touchdowns. During his last year with Pewaukee High School in 2012, he was an All-Conference quality player at quarterback, punter, and linebacker, and had 42 tackles and five sacks in his first year. As a tight end in his junior season, he caught 27 passes for 505 yards and three touchdowns. The six-foot-five, 244-pound youngest Watt was redshirted in 2013 and missed the entire 2014 season due to an injury. So far in the 2015 season, T.J. has played as an outside linebacker and has had a few tackles here and there coming off of the bench. His first solo tackle came on September 19, 2015, in a 28-3 home win over the Troy Trojans. His season high currently sits at two tackles on October 10, 2015 during a close 23-21 win visiting the Nebraska Cornhuskers. Time will only tell if T.J. will have a potential future playing in the NFL as well, which is why it will be interesting to see if his playing time and statistics will increase in his junior and senior seasons playing at Camp Randall Stadium.

On another interesting note, J.J. Watt does have a LinkedIn account, which is a social media website designed to allow professionals to build a network online. While he lists two current jobs as defensive end for the Houston Texans – where his job duties include making sure the opposing quarterbacks "have a very, very bad day" – you may find that he is also the vice president of power relations for Reliant Energy. It seems that the position was created more as a marketing tool to allow Watt to be able to be the face of Reliant's brand, which would join a long list of other big name brands that Watt is a spokesperson for, including Gatorade, Reebok, American Family Insurance, and Ford. Reliant Energy is a subsidiary company under NRG Energy Inc., a U.S. energy company that uses Reliant to provide retail electric services in the state of Texas. While Watt might not be an actual vice president where he does paperwork in a private office and goes to board meetings with a suit, tie, and briefcase in hand, he definitely feels it warrants being included in his work experience on his LinkedIn resume. Maybe after his career playing in the NFL ends down the road, he might consider entering the world of business.

Chapter 6: J.J. Watt's Impact on Football and Beyond

J.J. Watt has always strived to not only be a great NFL player, he's also wanted to someone who can use football as a way to give to other kids and be a positive role model. There were role models for Watt when he was growing up, so why shouldn't he pay it forward to today's youth?

Among the charitable work he does, being able to have different types of interactions with children who are sick with life-threatening diseases is among one of Watt's favorites. Most recently, on October 14, 2015, Watt was all dressed up as Gotham City's finest for a Halloween party at the Texas Children's Hospital in Houston, Texas. Watt was dressed in a full Batman cape and cowl while speaking in a grizzly Batman voice similar to the one used by Christian Bale in *The Dark Knight* film trilogy. It was just the most recent example of Watt spending time with youths while signing autographs, playing foosball, and decorating pumpkins along with the children.

The thing about being an active member of the community is that it will often be recognized by your team and the league as a whole. Back on August 26, 2014, Watt received the "Spirit of the Bull" community award during a team luncheon, becoming the fourth Houston Texan to receive the honor. The Texans like to recognize their players doing things like visiting children who are ill and work on a number of projects to help different types of people in the community. Later that season, Watt was nominated by the team for the 2014 NFL Salute to Service Award that is given to a player, coach, or owner who focuses on helping to provide support to active and veteran service members of the U.S. military and all branches of the Armed Forces. Watt was an obvious choice for many events, meeting with service members and even showing his support on his sleeves and gloves in pregame warm-ups with camouflage equipment. He also made a trip to visit Army Soldiers who were stationed at the Regional Command South that was set up in the Middle East back in March 2013. The award would eventually go to Chicago Bears defensive end Jared Allen for his work in his Homes 4 Wounded Warriors Foundation.

While he hasn't won the award for his ways of honoring the military, he still shows his support, even going as far as to write a lengthy post on his Facebook page about how the real heroes are those who fight overseas and defend the country, not a defensive end in a football uniform making millions. He also stated that football players and other professional athletes in general don't deserve "the worship that we often receive" and that football is just a game.

"It is not life or death. We are not going off to war, we are not putting our lives on the line, we are not protecting our country's freedom. But we are in the headlines ...it is only right that we honor the true heroes of this country ..." Watt wrote on his Facebook page.

Additionally, when someone plays with the dominance that Watt has had in recent years, the athlete in question is likely going to start popping up on television and in other advertisements away from the football field. In early 2015, Watt was one of the key components of the advertising campaign for Gatorade's 50th anniversary. He has also been seen in other commercials for Bose headphone, Papa John's pizza, and American Family Insurance; some are funny and some are more on the serious side. In an interview with SI.com, Watt said that he is grateful for being involved in fun advertisements as long as he is allowed to do them in his way, a way that will keep his family and loved ones proud.

One of the things that most professional athletes like to do after becoming established in their careers is to use some of their fame for the good. A number of superstars have invested in a number of charities and others have used some of their name recognition to build a foundation that can help an important cause that they feel needs attention to improve their communities. Some will help promote other established organizations like the Make-A-Wish Foundation, while other star athletes want to help raise money for medical research towards things like cancer. For Watt, his focus was to provide youths opportunities to achieve their athletic goals, especially for those who have the same type of desires to do what Watt was able to do.

If you go to the official website for the Justin J. Watt Foundation, there is a message from the NFL superstar about how he hopes to make fans proud of him for his work off of the field with the focus of helping youths find similar opportunities like the ones he received as a small-town kid from Wisconsin who simply wanted to play for the Wisconsin Badgers college football team and eventually the NFL.

His foundation is a recognized 501c(3) nonprofit organization that is currently working with several middle schools located in the states of Texas and Wisconsin, as well as other schools across the rest of the country that don't have the proper funding to be able to provide students with various after-school athletics and activities. Watt's foundation is focused on helping schools to be able to provide the activities that can keep youths in a safe environment that keeps them involved in something positive, while also teaching lessons that can be carried with them for the rest of their lives. The foundation's website – jjwfoundation.org – notes that having these activities will also teach youths to be able to work together as a team while also learning how to advance past adversity, as well as about what a little bit of hard work will do to help find success in just about every situation imaginable.

In the end, the goal is to make sure that sports are used as a way to help improve lives and to build character that carries forward over time. Children should have big dreams, just like Watt did when he was in grade school. It could have been a much easier path to the NFL if there were some activities and support for players like Watt. The foundation was formed in 2010 and in the first five years has donated more than $1 million to help different school sports programs. The support comes in the form of things like providing uniforms and equipment to middle school age children. For a school to qualify to receive support from the J.J. Watt Foundation, that have to have at least 40 percent of their students qualifying to receive free or reduced lunch assistance. Other things the foundation requires is that the equipment purchased must be long-term equipment that is designed to last for more than just a year. Other than that, the money is allowed to be used for any athletic activity – including football, basketball, baseball, soccer, cheerleading, rugby, and many more sports. Watt remembers being able to wear his jersey through the halls of school on a Friday before a big game, which brought a sense of pride. While a majority of the schools the foundations supports mainly schools in the states of the teams Watt has played for (Wisconsin, Texas), funds have also been sent to schools that meet the above-mentioned qualifications in states like Alabama, California, Illinois, and Indiana.

The foundation has also raised money by having an annual J.J. Watt Charity Classic held at Constellation Field in Sugar Land, Texas. The event includes a home run derby and a softball game where you see the offensive and defensive players from the Houston Texans face each other for a fun contest for bragging rights. It has been a very successful event that has helped raise nearly $1 million since the inaugural game in 2013. The only problem the foundation has ever had is being able to find the schools who could use the funds made available to the foundation while also making sure they provide the necessary help so that the school can maintain the program without having to find money every year to keep the programs around longer.

The foundation is named after the Houston Texans defensive star who is part of the five-person board, but his mother Connie is also part of the decision-making as the foundation's vice president. They are part of the five-person group that makes decisions about which schools who have applied and have been able to show where the money would be going and their past invoices, and on getting an idea of how well their funds will be used by the schools to help support after-school activities that can benefit students to remain active when their parents are still working and unable to meet them at home after school.

Chapter 7: Watt's Legacy in the NFL

If you count the first half of the 2015 season, J.J. Watt has 345 total tackles in just under five seasons with the Houston Texans. Only 44 of those tackles were assisted – where someone joined in on the hit – while also getting about 68 and a half sacks that will likely continue to grow. He broke the previous record of 54 sacks once held by former Texan Mario Williams in 2014. Watt's career statistics also show well, having deflected 42 passes, forcing 13 total fumbles and two defensive returns for a touchdown (one interception, one fumble recovery) and one safety. Yet he has also scored in other ways, with three of his six career touchdowns in the 2014 season coming as a tight end on a goal line offense.

All of these numbers show why Watt is a three-time NFL Pro Bowl selection (2012-2014) as well as other accomplishments in his still young professional football career – four-time AFC Defensive Player of the Month (September 2012, December 2012, September 2014 and September 2014); three-time first-team NFL All-Pro selection (2012-2014); three-time Defensive Player of the Year through *Pro Football Focus* (who also named him to the top of the 101 Best Player of the Year List in the same time frame, 2012-2014); three-time All-AFC Team by the Pro Football Writers of America (2012-2014); two-time AFC Defensive Player of the Year (2012, 2014); and two-time NFL Defensive Player of the Year (2012, 2014).

Watt was a runner-up for the NFL Most Valuable Player Award after the 2014 season, which went to Green Bay Packers quarterback Aaron Rodgers, who had 4,381 passing yards, 38 touchdown passes and a completion rate of 65.6 percent. Still, it's hard to tell someone who had 78 tackles, 20 and a half sacks and five total touchdowns on both sides of the ball that they shouldn't be named the MVP of the league.

Rodgers had 32 of the 50 votes with Watt having only 13 votes. Watt wasn't completely empty-handed in 2014, as he won the Bert Bell Award, which is awarded by the Maxwell Football Club for their annual professional football player of the year. Watt joins a list of recipients that include Johnny Unitas, Walter Payton, Lawrence Taylor and Peyton Manning. It is interesting to note that Watt was the first defensive lineman to receive the award since defensive tackle Merlin Olsen with the Los Angeles Rams in 1974. Since then, it has mostly been the usual faces of the NFL with quarterbacks and running backs like Marshall Faulk and Adrian Peterson.

Watt likely still has another five or six good years of playing as the dominant defensive end and could also set additional new records. For example, he is the NFL's first ever player to have two seasons with 20 or more quarterback sacks and he could easily get at least a third, or even a fourth. On the all-time sacks list, Watt is 82nd with his 68.5 and will likely surpass players like Clay Matthews (69.5; 1978-1996) and Peter Boulware (70; 1997-2005) to reach the top 80. Depending on how long Watt plays in the NFL, he still has a ways to go to get to the top of the all-time sacks list with Bruce Smith having had 200 total sacks between 1985 and 2003, followed by Reggie White with 198 sacks accumulated between 1985 and 2000. Yet there's nothing really stopping Watt from reaching those numbers if he does play for another 10 seasons. So far, he seems to be able to keep himself healthy, having not missed a single start in the NFL and holding a 75-game streak as of this writing before December 2015.

Additionally, it might be tough for a defensive end like Watt to top the all-time list on tackles, which is held by former Atlanta Falcon linebacker Jessie Tuggle with 1,640 total tackles between 1987 and 2000. It could be possible he becomes the highest rated defensive end and surpasses Rickey Jackson who had 1,173 between defensive end and linebacker between

1983 and 1996 for the Atlanta Falcons, Buffalo Bills and Minnesota Vikings.

However, if there's anything that we've learned from watching Watt develop from his humble beginnings in Pewaukee, Wisconsin, to the national stage in Houston, Texas, and other NFL cities, we've learned not to assume that anything is impossible with Watt. There's been the common cliché that anything is possible with the proper amount of hard work, dedication, and determination. J.J. Watt is literally a walking definition of that old saying when it is put to the test. Just ask Andrew Luck, Matt Hasselbeck, and other quarterbacks who have had to consistently deal with him year in and year out in the NFL. He will likely greet any new rookie quarterbacks who were thinking of making an impact before meeting the defensive juggernaut for the Texans.

All of these numbers and awards will likely help him earn a spot to be enshrined at the Professional Football

Hall of Fame in Canton, Ohio. Sure, injuries can happen to anyone regardless of star power and there's never any guarantees for success and earning that final honor to join other great linemen like Walter Jones and Bruce Williams. It will all be pending how many more number he puts up as a defensive end, or if he continues to score touchdowns as a tight end for extra credit. The one thing we haven't seen in the last few years is any signs that Watt might be slowing down as he finishes up his fifth season in the NFL. It could be awhile, as long as he continues to keep his body and mind healthy and fresh, which would be bad news for the other 31 quarterbacks who have to see him across the line of scrimmage. If all of that happens, there's no doubt that Watt will find himself in Canton with just being on the voting ballot once.

Watt has been what seems to be a perfect blend of athleticism, charisma and character. He's not going to show up in the news for having illegal firearms, drugs, or other items of crime that have been found among other good players who aren't always what they try to appear to be. Watt is also been someone who has never been busted for performance-enhancing drugs, nor has he been connected to deflating footballs or having opposing teams' practices video recorded. Watt is almost like the prototypical jock, but without any negative baggage. For the most part, he keeps his nose clean and surrounds himself with his family, good-natured friends and his teammates. He also remains active in the communities near Houston, Texas, where he plays professional football and back at home near Pewaukee, Wisconsin. This fact might frustrate some people who might get sick and tired of hearing about everything positive that Watt is doing, waiting for the other shoe to drop.

With five season in the NFL, it hasn't. Nor are there any signs of there being a second shoe that might bring unfortunate news about one of the newest faces of not only the Houston Texans, but also the National Football League. Part of that could be credited to his upbringing with a father who was a firefighter and served his community in southeastern Wisconsin and his mother, who was a supportive parent who waited for him to come home after school and football practice. There's the traditional saying about how it can sometimes take a village to raise a family.

When growing up in a small town like Pewaukee, Wisconsin, there's a very good chance that the majority of town knows about you. His teachers were the ones who kept telling him to reach for the stars and to never stop pursuing his goals of becoming not only a star with the Wisconsin Badgers football team, but also eventually in the NFL – although many of them probably hoped he would have been a star for the Green Bay Packers. Watt was given the tools to work his way to becoming a better student, which helped him do well at studying as an undergrad with a masters in life sciences and communication. Watt was eventually given the physical tools through his football team at Pewaukee High School, the same school that also developed his younger brothers Derek and T.J. into current Wisconsin Badger football players.

In the end, there are some people who question whether J.J. Watt is possibly too good to be true. What skeptics mean by that is that is that they question how someone can be such a dominant player and be able to handle being a spokesperson for several multi-million dollar companies and still be as active as he is with his own foundation for children while also showing support for sick kids and military service members. It's almost like the new contract hasn't changed his demeanor or opinion, all it seems to have done is make him have a bigger bank account and be able to buy a home with plenty of land so he can live in peace when he's not playing football.

Brian T. Smith of the Houston Chronicle wrote about that skepticism in a column in September 2015 where he considers Watt to be one of the most well-adjusted, sincere and genuine 26-year-olds in the world. "We want our sports heroes to be real, generous, caring human beings," Smith writes. "Watt is. And he's so real some get hurt."

It all comes down to what a professional athlete does when he reaches a certain level of fame in the world of sports. Does he or she let the fame and fortune go to their respective heads and inflate their ego? Or does the athlete in question harness both fame and fortune for the powers of good?

In the unique case of J.J. Watt, he has most certainly done things the right way, a way that is often taught in vain to other young athletes when they are in high school, college, or that first rookie mini-camp that teams hold to test out their new acquisitions. Watt is likely going to retire, at the very least, as one of the most real professional sports stars there has ever been. And that's because he's likely going to continue playing as hard, fast, and viciously as possible to maintain his dominance in the NFL. Afterwards, he will be just as likely to go live in that log cabin that he purchased earlier in this year and live on his large plot of land where he can focus on his family. There isn't anything that he has done that would prove otherwise, and maybe that's another reason he will be remembered by football fans.

Final Word/About the Author

I was born and raised in Norwalk, Connecticut. Growing up, I could often be found spending many nights watching basketball, soccer, and football matches with my father in the family living room. I love sports and everything that sports can embody. I believe that sports are one of most genuine forms of competition, heart, and determination. I write my works to learn more about influential athletes in the hopes that from my writing, you the reader can walk away inspired to put in an equal if not greater amount of hard work and perseverance to pursue your goals. If you enjoyed *J.J. Watt: The Inspiring Story of One of Football's Greatest Defensive Ends.* please leave a review! Also, you can read more of my works on *Colin Kaepernick, Aaron Rodgers, Peyton Manning, Tom Brady, Russell Wilson, Michael Jordan, LeBron James, Kyrie Irving, Klay Thompson, Stephen Curry, Kevin Durant, Russell Westbrook, Anthony Davis, Chris Paul, Paul George, Blake Griffin, Kobe Bryant,*

Joakim Noah, Scottie Pippen, Carmelo Anthony, Kevin Love, Grant Hill, Tracy McGrady, Vince Carter, Patrick Ewing, Karl Malone, Tony Parker, Allen Iverson, Hakeem Olajuwon, Reggie Miller, Michael Carter-Williams, John Wall, James Harden, Tim Duncan, and *Steve Nash* in the Kindle Store. If you love basketball, check out my website at claytongeoffreys.com to join my exclusive list where I let you know about my latest books and give you lots of goodies.

Like what you read? Please leave a review!

I write because I love sharing the stories of influential people like J.J. Watt with fantastic readers like you. My readers inspire me to write more so please do not hesitate to let me know what you thought by leaving a review! If you love books on life, basketball, or productivity, check out my website at claytongeoffreys.com to join my exclusive list where I let you know about my latest books. Aside from being the first to hear about my latest releases, you can also download a free copy of *33 Life Lessons: Success Principles, Career Advice & Habits of Successful People*. See you there!

Clayton

References

"J.J. Watt." *NFL.com*. N.p., n.d. Web.

"J.J. Watt NFL Football Statistics | Pro-Football-Reference.com." *Pro-Football-Reference.com*. N.p., n.d. Web.

"J.J. Watt." College Football at *Sports-Reference.com*. N.p., n.d. Web. .

Ganguli, Tania. "The life and times of J.J. Watt." *Ultimate Texans*. N.p., 13 Oct. 2012. Web.

Oates, Tom. "Oates: Watt's Decision to Leave Early is the Right Move." *Madison.com*. N.p. 7 Jan. 2011. Web.

Merrill, Elizabeth. "J.J. Watt – Mayberry and Mayhem." *ESPN*. ESPN Internet Venutures, n.d. Web.

"NFL Events: Combine Player Profiles – J.J. Watt." *NFL Events: Combine Player Profiles – J.J. Watt*. N.p., n.d. Web.

McKenna, Thomas. "J.J. Watt's New Contract Makes Him the League's Highest Paid Non-Quarterback." *The Huffington Post*. TheHuffingtonPost.com, n.d. Web.

"Can J.J. Watt One Day Be Like Mike? It's Not out of the Question." *SI.com*. N.p., n.d. Web.

Clements, Ron. "Texans DE J.J. Watt Has a New Job: VP of Power Relations." *Sporting News*. N.p., 22 July 2015. Web.

Schumacher, Ashley. "My Three Sons: Badger Mom Proud of Watt Brothers On, Off the Field." *Wisconsin Alumni Association*. N.p., 24 Aug. 2014. Web.

"Pacers' Aaron Rodgers Named Most Valuable Player." *NFL.com*. N.p., n.d. Web.

"J.J. Watt Football Recruiting." *ESPN.com*. N.p., n.d. Web.

"Recruiting Database: 2007 ESPN Top Defensive Ends." *ESPN*. ESPN Internet Ventures, n.d. Web.

"Facebook." *JJ Watt*. N.p., n.d. Web.

Smith, Brian T. "Some May Think J.J. Watt Seems Too Good to be True, but he has proven that he's genuine." *Houston Chronicle*. N.p., 11 Sept. 2015. Web.

Wilson, Aaron. "Texans Defensive End J.J. Watt Embraces Challenge against Undefeated Bengals." *Ultimate Texans*. N.p., 11 Nov. 2015. Web.